BROOM
BROOM

BROOM BROOM

Brecken Hancock

Coach House Books | Toronto, Ontario

first edition

Published with the generous assistance of the Canada Council for the
Arts and the Ontario Arts Council. Coach House also acknowledges the
support of the Government of Canada through the Canada Book Fund
and the Government of Ontario through the Ontario Book Publishing
Tax Credit.

LIBRARY AND ARCHIVES CANADA CATALOGUING IN PUBLICATION

Hancock, Brecken
    Broom Broom / Brecken Hancock – First edition.

Poems.
Issued in print and electronic formats.
ISBN 978 1 55245 288 2 (PBK) – ISBN 978 1 77056 379 7 (EPUB)

    I. Title.

PS8615.A5527B76 2014   C811'.6   C2013-907668-9

Purchase of the print version of this book entitles you to a free digital
copy. To claim your ebook of this title, please email sales@chbooks.com
with proof of purchase or visit chbooks.com/digital. (Coach House
Books reserves the right to terminate the free digital download offer at
any time.)

for The Moms

CONTENTS

I will go back to the great sweet mother,
Mother and lover of men, the sea.
I will go down to her, I and none other,
Close with her, kiss her and mix her with me.

Victorian
Poet

– Swinburne

Mommy, I'd rather have you dead than crazy.

– Yoko Ono

PROLOGUE

BEFORETIMES. Uranus culls his gilded camels and bathes in the Baikal, the Zaysan, the Lanao. He wades in low-lying plains, spas in every rain-filled meteor crater. Sixty-fourth parallel, March. Sunlight fires a salvo off his lover's collarbone. Gaia's slums hoard water, Asmat mud and patches of pubic forest. Her valleys are aqueducts feeding antechambers of lakes: caravans of bathtubs clawing overland talon by talon according to deep time, glacial wake, geochemistry. Lake Agassiz Basin. Morass hollow, calderas. Gathering my hair off the pillow, I rise from the spill on our sheets to bathe. Oceanus – Titan of the brutish Atlantic, master of Ketos and Kraken, conductor of sky to land. Half-man, half-serpent; horizon marks the fix. Biceps of accumulated cloud ceiling the sea. He'll rip your ship apart for a violin. His tail's a woman's braid dropped deep. And over its mucus and muscled carbuncles, legions of mollusc princes ascend, knot by knot by octopus tapas – crabs' pincers and half-spumed clams – through bergs of cloying oil slick, plagues of dross, black-blooming purple and a drowned Cassiopeia of phosphor. *Abyssss.* Germs fermenting in the kegs of their slow-moving shells. Up through the punch-holes of Poseidon's belt, out through the tunnels of his prosthetic manifold, svelte pipelines, immaculate taps – an invertebrate army comes to kiss the slit where my tail splits, two legs.

BRECKEN

Booze tides me.
TV abides me.

My tits slung
astride me,

I noose quiet
to lie with me.

My other husband's
a broom.

HUSHA

Some animals eat their young.
Animals sweet on their young.
Sh shh, sleep, little ones.

Carson says fetal sharks scarf
each other to abortion. Yum yum
in Mom's womb. It's on YouTube.

Lance says male dolphins will gang
rape a lady dolphin to death. Stuff her
blowhole, can't take a breath.

Tucky whispers, *Your cousin fucked
a bunny*. But I can't imagine
enough room in her tummy.

SANDY

Her bed gown brides her.
She's dumb as a broom.
Her quiets swim inside her.

Daddy can't shut-eye her
boggled doll peekaboo.
Her bed gown brides her.

We can't identify her
as Sandy, per se. She's make-do.
Her quiets swim inside her.

Ghouls queue to ride her.
Oozing like a fistula,
her bed gown brides her.

Mother's meat's in a wilder
chaos, but she got her due.
Her quiets swim inside her.

I'll smother her if I find her
inside me. Monkey see? *I do.*
I do. Her bed gown brides her
toward quiet. I swim inside her.

LAKE EFFECT

Snow blinds the deer hearse.
Snow needles the blood purse.
Snow porridge in the hobo's bowl.
Snow angels spread for ripper's toll.

Dormers dripping toilet paper.
Castles of albino crows.
Amniotic impersonator.
Vomit stipples Mommy's clothes.

Come snow, come sleep,
Bleach our red curtains
To surrender. O molester,
Put the animals to bed.

Bed the trees;
Rid us of forecast.
Calm the alabaster
Masts of dream.

Come dream, snow,
Bear in the cavern,
Rat in the cistern.
Every little chit in its hole.

Make us kid-glove clean again,
Intestines fresh from the fast.
Lay out your skin to swaddle our feet,
Snow madonnas maquillaged in ash.

WINTER, FRONTAL LOBE

Dark where Dad chops a hole.
Tunk. Dark hair blighted
by snow bees, his axe
trepanning the tarn's top.
Beneath what's frozen
slighted bodies blob up
from the din. Kraken, Leviathan,
the pail in my hand's a cauterized
aluminum stump.

Heave-ho to make the lake
gawp up at us. Heave again
to plunge the bucket
benthic deep.

Leave down the glum machine
(my arm-and-pail rocking-horse rig).
Winter's everywhere profusion.
Huddle over its sink:
head congested, festooned
with weeds. Mother is nuts.
The mind's an organ
of slush. *Ahusha.*
His axe can't cleave
this confusion.

haiku

SYMPTOMS INCLUDE DISINHIBITION

In lusting after
their son, Sandy remembers
her husband, young.

I'M ON A GIBBET, FONDLING MY FINE WORKMANSHIP

In the brume
of hangover
I dog-paddle
day. The oasis
of convalescence
appears solely
via nostalgia.
At the node
when I rake
back damp
hair, erosion
ratchets my gut.
Who's *tut-tutting*?
The bile
rinding my skin's
benign. In
every pang
a bullet of yin –
wine's its own
antidote. Beyond
its obvious notes,
oak, fog, neap
tide, daily bread –
alone at night,
I Sandy the bed.

MOM'S SISTERS' DAUGHTERS

Navy blue in the hall.
Five and five doors
and blue navy rising,
rising under the underslots.
Five and five doors framing ten rooms,
each with a woman in bed,
each with a woman sleeping.
Each with a yawning
window, each with a lamp, doused.
Across from each, a mirror.

▸▸

The navy's loud as wheezing. *Ah aha.*
Mountains climb beyond the window.
Ten and ten arms circling pillows,
not other bodies in their beds.
Ten and ten hands frigid with sweat.
Oceans rime beyond the window.
Women solo, tucked into themselves.
Rooms drenched in exhales.
The navy sounds, their breasts.
On thermals, birds beyond windows.

▸▸

A pug scrubs himself along carpet.
Room to room he marks
spurts of darkness
under each underslot.
Women's cheeks pillow-creased,
ten women ferning themselves.

Mouths *awe*
to navy tongues.

▸▸

Navy blue thick in the hall
as navy grackles, clotting. They hoist
their wings, gaw and fuffle
against each other, thick as piss
flooding under underslots.
The doors are slick with their cud and shit,
their tide under underslots.

▸▸

We women now bathing.
Off the hall, five and five knobs
to ten rooms, each with a woman in tub.
Ten women nailing mosquito bites,
scrubbing resin under ten and ten feet.
We sink into upside-down longing,
shave navy plumes off mounds.
The baths grow cold. We rise.
Our bodies rise to face mirrors.
Five and five mirrors,
twenty women facing ourselves.
Five and five mirrors now,
twenty women facing ourselves.
And through the walls
we face each other.
And through the walls
our backs to each other.
Aha. And in the mirror
twenty women. *Me?*

[1] In rare cases, tightly cemented sandstone constricts a stream, forcing water to carve in the only available direction: straight down. See Devil's Bathtub (post-Christian system of terms), Hocking Hills, Ohio.

[2] *Times Star.* Upland, CA, Oct. 30, 2007. Officials from the California Department of Food and Agriculture arrested a couple on felony cheese manufacturing charges after they were found with 375 pounds of illegally manufactured soft cheese at an outdoor market in San Bernardino County. They seized a variety of 'bathtub cheese,' as it is known on the street, including *panela, queso fresco* and *queso oaxaca.* Such cheese is a known health threat. Listeria causes miscarriage and stillbirth, premature delivery or infection of the newborn if ingested by a pregnant woman.

[3] The Mayans believed a woman's womb was a washtub that must never grow cold. If a chill in the uterus occurs, Mayan medicine advocates a hydrotherapy technique called the vaginal steam bath. Oregano, basil, marigold and rosemary are combined with boiling water and placed under a slotted chair. Naked from the waist down, the woman sits on the chair and covers herself with a blanket.

[4] A man becomes unclean when he discharges semen, whether asleep or awake, in large or small quantities, in lust or disgust. If a man has sexual intercourse with a woman and his penis enters either of her secret conduits up to the point of his circumcision, both people become unclean. If a man has sexual intercourse with an animal and semen comes out of his body, this is sufficient reason for him to take a bath.

[5] 250,000 bacteria per square inch: worn-out bathtubs are not only unsightly but also dangerous. Filth, micro-organisms and pathogens cache in millions of tiny pores that pock porcelain. No matter how vigorously you scour, it never comes clean.

[6] Bathtub Madonna (also known as Mary on the half shell) is an artificial grotto constructed by upending a clawfoot tub and half-burying it so that the exposed rim frames the virgin idol.

[7] *Time.* Cambridge, MA, Sept. 24, 1965. Prof. Ascher H. Shapiro, head of the Department of Mechanical Engineering at MIT, has finally proven that water drains counter-clockwise in the northern hemisphere. He constructed a perfectly symmetrical tub, filled it to the brim, applied a clockwise swirl, then let it sit for twenty-four hours in a void. Carefully pulling the plug, he filmed the results. Using Shapiro's technique, five persistent investigators at the University of Sydney have now duplicated his experiment,

demonstrating clockwise drainage Down Under. 'With the proper tub and reasonable patience,' Shapiro proposes, 'humans could have proven the rotation of the earth 1,000 years ago.'

[8] Much is made of the rental apartment's 'heinous pink bathroom fixtures.' Unable to extricate the basement suite's wretchedness from her own grief, Willa writes at length of her muddled creativity: 'My mind, too, seems submerged in the tub's brine and I cannot see what lies beyond the confines of its husk. Even monsters are only recombinations of things glimpsed lurking in the drain's eddies.' Later that year, after beginning a long-distance affair with Joseph Klein, the German photographer, her emailed letters rediscover the kite-flying tone characteristic of her juvenilia:

> I couldn't wait for you to get the mail! Has Wittgenstein's Tractatus Logico-Philosophicus *finally arrived? It flew across the world to be with you. From its past (unknown), to the UK book dealer, to my desk, to your bedchamber, its journey from copyright 1961 was arduous. You'll now read it in the bath.*

[9] *The New York Times*. Montreal, QC, Jan. 31, 1892. A sensational suicide occurred here to-night. At 8 o'clock a man named Thomas Bell left his family at supper and went up stairs to the bathroom, where, after locking the door, he laid down in the bath-tub and cut his throat from ear to ear, severing the windpipe and the left carotid artery. He was discovered by his ten-year-old daughter, who fainted at the sight, falling on the floor. No reason can be given for the mad act, as the suicide is supposed to have been in good circumstances and was not a drinking man.

[10] 70% of accidents at home occur in the bathroom. Drowning, burning, falling, poisoning, electrocution – the smallest room in the modern home is a veritable asps' nest of peril with its many electrical appliances near water; above-sink stash of prescription and over-the-counter drugs; under-sink horde of chemicals; slippery surfaces; and unforgiving materials such as ceramic, chrome and tile.

[11] One does not usually employ the bathroom to illustrate principles of mechanization, yet the exquisite transformation of plumbing facilities into their present proliferate variety aptly demonstrates human obsession with efficiency, aesthetics and automation. We shave over the sink, browse the soggy pages of home-reno magazines in the tub and sometimes have sex in the shower. Skin and hair leach down the drain; urine, vomit and feces flush down; our tears and red edges spiral, clean.

PROGRESSION BLUNTS EMPATHY

Hush now, Mama, don't
say a word. Daughter's gonna
drink until you're cured.

You loll enfolded in the civil fixtures of this world. *Mortar,*
pillar, spiral, stone. Architecture fosters the isolation your
body affords.

In unmoored clouds, in the towering emission: a face. *Dixie cup*
that gods tip to suck. You identify, and here you're human.

It's not for you to delimit space. *Arch, bridge, window, hollow.*
You search the bedroom for a face.

Enfolded in architecture, figments of progress furnished
by progression. *Lungen, from light.* To breathe, you see
by these lungs.

Infantries of row houses. You are a small doll in the corner
of a dark room. *Voice from the bed bled into the towering.*

You force everything to nest in recognizable shapes. *Mortar,*
hollow, archway, stair. You take the air, enfolded in symptoms
of the face.

Any instrument is a champed bit, a resonant reining-in. *Objects*
in mirror are farther than they appear. You always
hold you at arm's length.

THE NEAR SITE

Today I was consumed by an article telling me that a
centaur may have existed once – only briefly, and most
likely by accident. More of a monkey-mule than a human-
horse. I will devote the rest of my life to pursuing archae-
ological evidence of this beast.

           – J. D.

But you didn't. You told me the evidence
was femur in swamp, cold murder of a north
woman not fully sunk in a cedar stand
of false bottoms, her skull entwined in the root-
squirm of long-dissolved trees – the rest of her neat,
skin-stripped and frozen bones were five ladies' ghosts

gathered around a lamppost. Any real ghosts
shrank from you, asquat on top of evidence
that even taiga bogs aren't always neat
eaters. What's more, you knew full well how this north
swill that passes for wetland often takes root
in violence. Your numb feet had you flex, stand,

then wonder if we'd ever been made to stand
on four spindles, like horses, and whether ghosts
of equine flank, knee, fetlock and hoof still root
in our delicate joints. Lack of evidence
maintains the contrary, but there, amid north
quagmire, you considered evolution's neat

halfway solutions. Records skip. Far from neat,
there is room for something much like God to stand
and salve the join with spit. Or what of a north
creature? Half deer, half woman carved from snow? Ghosts
stirred within their graves of buried evidence.
How can archaeology help but to root

among a woman's thrown bones, seeking a route
by which we back into beasts? Not only neat
theories of ape-enhanced mules, but 'evidence'
too – bonobo-on-dorado, sewn to stand
as mermen – must spur hunts for Kentauride ghosts,
their tangled genes. By then, hands jammed up with north,

you were too stiff to zip. Rime and hoary north
gathered as quills across green fleece. Stomping, root-
wracked legs prickling with your weight, you let the ghosts
go. It wasn't woman, but deer remains. Neat
really, how similar the two, how they might stand
like kin. Just the eye socket's whole – evidence

that the north and its brines eat our aims, our neat
archive of finds. Root, no eye. From where we stand,
whatever the evidence, we know lampposts for ghosts.

INCUS, MALLEUS, STAPES

An unreachable beach crowned
with wigwams of whale ribs.
From above, the scattered scraps
are wrecked and stripped ships,
or giants' claws that, ossified, grope
for Xanadu now, grope now for
the fingers of women who taught them
the fingers of women.

Sand sifts, you and I canoe,
catch a jutting bar of shore.
Dock, years after these whales
came to die, to drone of insects.
No one knows what becomes of sound
when all the world's coquilles
hit shoal.

What's more, we'll string tin cans with twine
when we crave the tones of home.
We tear off our T-shirts
and jeans, you push me down,
stirrup foot atop foot atop
the ground. My teeth tap your wrist –
mammals on the water line. Your hammer,
this anvil of mine, we forge
into one another, pulse beat,
taste of iron, pelvis moulding
to palm. We hear woodpecker.

We hear *strike, strike-strike.*
You fashion me of ribs,
dress the tack of my skin.
All the while waves snuff out the castles,
the silhouettes of our children.
We don't stop, *don't stop.*

Preteens imagine being seen
naked someday, and present to the mirror.
Whales beach to finally see themselves.
Here, who'll tell what's left
of our workings, spilt hammocks,
the ossicles sundered from their ears?

WOMAN, *WOLF*

Predator, in whenever blue
I left you, I made light work of walking.

> *What the dogs bore when we offed them*
> *to separate homes was, until then, lost on me.*

West was decoy, Day-Glo,
a crowded *pensione.*
Your absence, that erasure itself,
became the action.

> *Every boy on a burro was a swordslinger.*
> *Yet, I couldn't parley a decent noonday ballet.*
> *Play isn't 'play' in the dog days.*

One riddle escorted me:
for an unspecified few, life's absent
of abject cruelty.

> *Your nightwear wakes me –*
> *I wedge windows ajar in all weather,*
> *and camisoles, mounted on curtain rods, quake.*

You cooed, 'Nobody knows we are together,'
or 'Peasants were together like this.'
My purple hands
crutched in your armpits.

> *Every sense but sight requires touch. The light*
> *in my eyes – how very large your departure.*

You were the bloom
in my aplomb.
The plastique
in my arboretum.

> *I sink apiece with the wine. My legs,*
> *slabs of burro meat beneath bedsheets.*

Love, you're the kind of cur
that gnaws the buttons off his coat
and drinks and drinks to blur the raw.

LIFE'S A CYCLE OF HAIRSTYLES

Husband leaves me.
I swill another.

Sandy cleaves me.
You only get one mother.

Best friends' babies
amass like cloud cover.

Why wasn't Mommy
a better lover?

DUOS

The hydra's violence regrows in twos.
In one version the cock crows twice.

To the Greeks, the Goths said *bar bar.*
Animals keep odd hours. Jekyll's double

prowls potato fields as a common white
moth. The same blue at dusk as at dawn.

I want you like Donne's stiff
twin compasses, cocked and fused.

Behind the Jews, Rome.
Twins spit from a wolf's tongue.

The first two times you call *wolf*
you'll be answered.

A cavity defines the size
of the speculum (instrument of space

rather than form). Romans wrote it
II. Everything's doppelgänger –

even the sun admires itself in a dead sphere.
Let me kiss your pillared lips,

the keystone between your knees; two times
V is X. Genital, and then

chromosomal. Boffin's True Mirror©
doesn't reverse its reflect.

Come again? Cro-Magnon,
evolver. The miracle of sight is inversion.

THE CRIME FOR WHICH HE'S SERVING LIFE

We manufacture wonder where we can.

Elephants bow to feline gods, lionize

what opens them. Aroused, a dog's

penis will bloom a grappling hook.

Colorectal surgeons kneel before the sphinx

of the sphincter. He was eighteen

when he committed the index offence:

cutting short another boy's killjoy scream.

He then inured himself to prison as a rigorous,

monotonous discipline, repeating the same

emotion for fifteen years. He's been diagnosed

for a lack of tears. Time's the crux.

This poem, his prom. I grew up with a boy

who grew into a murderer and I loved him. Love him

on the far side of the object of love,

the him beyond him. For words there are no

larger words. We all manufacture grandeur:

I don't believe in any god, so why am I

nodding toward something like a soul?

What does one live for? Are we appealing

as a species? Would I suffocate my colicky baby

to save the village from alien detection?

Is the goal here to eke out another clutch of years?

The fridge *oms* us asleep. Hours after the spat, Brother comes home to torpor and the calico's kibble scattered off the plate. His sandwich. The unremarkable wirefire whisk. Water-lit shapes *swip* against the walls like shades; he drips downstairs.

Accident 1: Fire! The popcorn's ablaze. Mom and Dad, out. Brother stabs through a box of baking soda, douses the stove – the kitchen's achoke with flocks of smoke. Flicking tea towels, we *whish* our genies out the flung door, the thrown-open winter window. We're Teflon. We're all the terrible glee.

Bluebottle fly *bunt bunts* against glass. In the alley, the hirsute shadow of a domestic animal against stucco. Our pets drowned by a boy somewhere in the suburban forest. *We miss you, Charlie, Sonja.*

Accident 2: Digger-upper of dead deer limbs finds the apple pie. Paws on the counter, Otis wolfs 60% of our dessert without spilling. Nearly sated, his poise slips when Mom flips the switch. Traitor under a spotlight and the pie-plate coin toss. Tails up the carpet loses.

Mom's broom, the *vroom vroom* of her vacuum. She torna-does from one corner to another, no eye in her storm-grey eyes. The houseflies lie petrified. Kitchen cabinets pop pill bottles like perfumeries.

Accident 3: Pepsi from the pantry escapes my grip – tars ceiling, walls, carpet. *Liquid without a container chooses its own vocation, Mother.* Still on the threshold, then she's on me with blades of windmill movement. A body's mass isn't equal to its presence; a body's just gist. The stain, the stain, the stain.

I focus on my weight and what sadness adheres to the mundane. Habit, be my guest: I hunt the animal inside myself, the self-eater, and lunch it to rest.

Accident 4: Sixteen; still a virgin. Stammer home at 4 AM, *If that meadowlark don't sing, I'm gonna taste Phil's filthy thing.* O, but here's Mom, crusted to counters' corner. By stovelight, mills my ring in the blender.

Dad rips up the carpet; goodbye, stains.

Accident 5: Slap across the face; my nosebleed confettis ceramic tile. And then I'm out the door, bare feet breaking through the hardened heaps of snow behind our house. *To flay a little rabbit skin to wrap my baby bunt ... bunt,* my gut-moths against the window. Through the looking glass, I watch her frenetic smear.

Mockingbird bought me a mama. By its waggish voodoo, her head's on backwards.

Accident 6: Foot hiked up on marble countertop, I violin-bow a boning blade against my right calf to find the deep carpet of white. During her brain autopsy, they'll find Pick bodies – protein tangles or ballooned neurons. These beautiful silver-staining spherical aggregations.

LAG

Grief is a door, strange how feral. It locks
twice, tooth-in-tooth against the jamb, and seals
this house – oneiric shell where all of Bach
digests at once. Top stair: a cockatiel-
headed angel bobs to ten by each climb
of the clock. Thirteenth floor, Mommy can't sleep.
Turn in turn she loses time; legs entwine
in bedsheets. This door – dimensional pleat
between us – as simple as the desire
to pass through. But *no*, there's a debt she owes
the farther side. Agape, affixed, afire,
it doesn't matter. And even though
her body's lying near, I can't hear my mom.
I fear what she feels. I pray that she's numb.

FORGETTING BEGETS BEGETS

Suckling Sandy's milky
wastewater. A daughter's
a womb entombed.

MOUNT SAPO

Let us bathe in gold
as long as we suspire.
As we supple, froth. Longitude
as longing, epithelial
as slough. We pumice
as lathing, limbs
as latitudes, as silver.
As we whittle, let us nuzzle.
As we dip, rupture
as bloodlines. Tubs
or abattoirs, let us breathe.
As we're hairless, lolly.
As we bubble, dizzy.
As our mirrors mirage,
let us wraith.
As we christen, we cure
as leather, lard
as lather. We launder
as immolation, as ashes ashes.
As long as rapture, chasm.
As we cannibal, plume,
as curtains of sud juices.
As we wet, let us doctor
or mob Diana's stag.
As nudists, let us watch.
As we erotic, tourniquet.
As we tear, Bacchus. As long
as we asphyxiate, let us ecstasy.
As we rubber, we drizzle

as sodden gold tailings.
As mice to laughter's wife.
As we esophagus, *chop chop*.
As long as we sarcophagus,
let us bathe.

3300 BCE: Copper pipes snake beneath an Indus palace. Sewage systems and democratic access to public wells ensure two millennia of peace.

2500 BCE: Nascent plumbers in Mesopotamia experiment with clay mixed into shredded straw. Bitumen tars conduits and stopgap plugs. After finding his brindled whippet drowned in a tub of crude oil, King Gilgamesh orders the first public execution by tar and feather.

2475 BCE: Egyptians install bathing chambers and lavatories in the Abusir tombs. Pharaoh Sahure employs mummified falcons, ibises and cats as water-bearers in the afterlife. The naked mole rat goes blind living exclusively underground.

1795 BCE: To seduce his wife and celebrate their first wedding anniversary, Hephaestus designs a cast-iron talonfoot. Custodian of *techne*, Hephaestus forwards both technique and technology. He is admired as an artist and wright but reviled as a labourer and a cripple. Weeks later, catching Ares at her taps, Hephaestus ensnares the adulterers in the tub's sister invention: an unbreakable chain-link shower curtain, so fine it's invisible.

1200 BCE: The wet dream of immortality. Thetis dips Achilles in the Styx.

1195 BCE: Linear B records an ancient name for the personal bathtub: *re-wo-te-re-jo*. After serving as a ritual fixture, the Larnax tub bears a corpse across the sea to the afterlife.

Minoans boast elaborate aqueducts, hot and cold running taps, and sewage systems that accommodate a prototypical flush toilet. They bathe and bury in the same vessel.

1183 BCE: Clytemnestra guts Agamemnon in the bath. His final berth is a skiff fashioned of fingernails pitched down a river of urine. Sky whips him like Clytemnestra's crop of black hair. Albino giants on grave mounds guard the east bank, awaiting redress for the sacrifice of his daughter.

1046 BCE: Warriors of the Zhou Dynasty observe rituals of hair washing to preserve honour in battle. In one famous tale, Confucius visits Lao-tzu while the latter curtains his hair over a scabbard to dry.

603 BCE: King Nebuchadnezzar of Babylon crawls like a vole through the dust. For seven years he lives with beasts, tearing and eating his own skin. God tortures him with dementia, body lice, swampy testicles and incontinence. In every bracken bush he sees a nightjar, the psychopomp's familiar, come to chirr him down to the Great Below. Finally pardoned for his sin of arrogance and allowed to live, he returns to the Hanging Gardens where slaves sluice the filth from his body, scrubbing him with soap congealed from goat blubber and cremation ash.

500 BCE: Ornate baths rise as key fixtures of Roman architecture. Urban citizens daily visit any one of many public thermæ; private balnea in wealthy homes resemble shallow swimming pools and encompass entire rooms. Romans effectively avoid plague by creating a complex sanitation system that hurries sewage from the city in bronze pipes.

350 BCE: The Hohokam, in what is now Arizona, dig trenches and build pipelines using bored-out logs that shuttle irrigation over two hundred miles. Leaks quench slugs, bulbs, berries and weedy fronds. Spotted across the Sonaran Desert, a blotch of javelina cabbage burgeons at every chink.

343 BCE: Nectanebo II, last native ruler of Egypt, flees to Nubia following the Persian invasion, leaving behind what would have been his sarcophagus. Later installed as a ritual bath in a mosque, the green breccia box is inscribed with extracts from the book of Imi-duat, a historical record of kings and priests, not to be confused with the book of Amduat (*That Which Is in the Afterworld*).

232 BCE: Mathematician, astronomer and inventor Archimedes stumbles onto a method for gauging the volume of irregular objects. Stepping into the bath, he spots water rise counter to the submersion of his body. According to rumour, he sprints naked through the streets of Syracuse, proclaiming either 'God has given me the answer!' or '*I have found it!*'

63 BCE: Augustus Caesar commissions an artificial lake, eighteen hundred feet by twelve hundred feet, where criminals and slaves stage *navalia proelia*, simulated sea battles. By Nero's time, theatrical water wars utilize up to nineteen thousand men and over a hundred ships. Drowning bulls dog-paddle through bile-blooming blue, the floating button mushrooms of men's overbrimmed fat, and the chum of their own blood.

28 CE: John the Baptist dips Jesus in the Jordan. From shore, Joseph replays his recurring wet nightmare: Mary becomes pregnant from sperm in the caldarium.

300 CE: Farmers between Ilminster and Bath maintain a sarcophagus as a horse trough. Resting in a backyard garden, the marble fixture depicts the life of Jonah, said to be reborn from the belly of a monster. The front offers three time-lapse engravings: first, Jonah's boat, tossed at sea, awaits the tentacled embrace of Ketos; second, Ketos vomits Jonah onto an island; and finally, the hero reclines safely against a tree hoisting a gourd of mead, his arm around a peacock.

415 CE: Anxious that nudity nurtures licentiousness, early Christian fathers preach against public bathing. Washing is condoned for cleanliness, but not recreation. Extensive renovations convert a Roman bathhouse into the Basilica of Santa Pudenziana – pools become baptismal fonts, lounging benches, pews. The Latin *creatio*, 'creation from nothing', applies specifically to the potency of God. Architects and other artists are mere imitators or converters, never inventors. Cassiodorus writes, 'Things made and created differ, for we can make who cannot create.'

625 CE: Gaozu, inaugural emperor of the Tang Dynasty, bequeaths his bathing tub as a palace legacy. The tub's engraved aphorism buoys the twenty-two emperors to come with a lesson of change and renovation: 'Every day, make thyself new. Day by day, make thyself new, and new again, and new again, and forever new.'

900 CE: Mayans plumb the first pressurized water feature in the new world and inscribe tubs with an astrological cartography, atlas to the waterways of beyond.

1348 CE: Forty-five percent of Europe's population succumbs to the Black Death. Bathing, thought to transmit disease through the pores of the body, begins to decline as common practice. One hundred and fifty years later, Queen Isabella of Castile boasts at having bathed only twice in her lifetime: once at birth and once on her wedding day.

1611 CE: Hungarian countess Erzsébet Báthory perfects the iron maiden. Over six hundred teenaged virgins wilt in the metal coffin, organs bored, blood spilling out a grate in the bottom. Báthory bathes in their juices to preserve her youth. In one famous story, she consults with King Matthias while fanning her honour over the pillow to dry.

1627 CE: The Witch Trials in Bamberg, Germany, are the most extensive in Europe. Prince-Bishop Gottfried Johann Georg Fuchs von Dornheim establishes a firm of full-time torturers and builds Drudenhaus, a dedicated witch prison to house the special appliances that deal with the damned. Children as young as six months are ritually dunked in ice-cold baths and scorched in tubs of lime. The wealthiest citizens fall victim to the hunt, their assets and property confiscated as Dornheim and his officers grow wealthy and porcine. Although the accused never escape eventual burning at the stake, Dornheim popularizes a pithy slogan by which he justifies the intermediate torture: 'We drown the witch within to let the Christian live.'

1793 CE: With quill and paper in hand, Jean-Paul Marat soaks in a cold tub to soothe the itchy explosions that crater his skin. Charlotte Corday stabs him there, leaving the knife's mast to hoist the red flag of his chest. Marat's vessel, a ship of French Revolutionaries' fingernails, ferries him through the sewers of Paris. Rats with facial tumours sentinel the west bank. Living exclusively underground, they've gone blind.

1843 CE: *Rub-a-tug-tug. Three hung men in a tub.*

1846 CE: Cholera epidemics and the germ theory of contagion lead to the Public Baths and Wash Houses Act in England. Governments provide the working class facilities to keep clothes and bodies clean.

1847 CE: The royal bathing machine, a green weatherboard carriage on large black wheels, is built at Osborne House on the Isle of Wight. Most contraptions of the time are horse-drawn: chestnut-deep in the surf, Clydesdales are brought around to face the shore. Inside the cabana even the most refined female can change into a bathing costume and then descend by a few steps out the back – the machine completely blocking any public view. Queen Victoria's modern ramp-and-winch system, powered by steam engine (and complete with plumbed toilet), allows her to trundle into the shallows and dip while maintaining her modesty. After her first excursion, she confides to her journal: 'Drove to the beach with my maids in the machine. I undressed and bathed in the sea (for the first time in my life!). I thought it delightful till I put my head under water – and thought I would be stifled by all the black water of England.'

1872 CE: The Ku Klux war in North Carolina shuts down the Mars Hill College campus. One KKK ballad, later found hand-scrawled in the college's archives, sneers at Rueben Manning Deaver who reportedly hid in his bathtub to avoid a rub-a-scrub-scrub at the hands of the Klan.

1890 CE: According to an ancient Russian proverb, a woman in a tub is a room within a room. Sponging his wife's pregnant belly, Sergey Malyutin conceives the first matryoshka doll.

1891 CE: No sooner has the bathtub become a fixture in the working-class home than it offers a common altar for suicide. In Halifax, seventeen-year-old Thomas Drake breaks into his neighbours' house to slit his wrists. The Smiths find him alive, reclining in a tub infused with blood, petting their cat Teddy perched on the edge.

1909 CE: Three-hundred-and-forty-pound William Howard Taft becomes lodged in the White House bathtub, nearly missing his inauguration. When the story surfaces in the media years later, Taft's supporters attempt to discredit the rumours by pointing to a revealing symmetry: the President and his Justice Department had dissolved the Bathtub Trust, a cartel of porcelain makers bent on creating a price-fixing monopoly to control the sale of bathtubs and toilets.

1917 CE: Controversy rocks the bathing world when H. L. Mencken publishes a completely inaccurate account of bathing and bathtub history.

1920 CE: *Bathtub gin*, a vile bootleg solution to prohibition, explodes onto the U.S. market. Homicide rises by 12.7%; battery by 13.2%. John Dillinger bathes in banknotes both before and after bottles of whiskey.

1925 CE: From the froth of her tub, gin in hand, Zelda Fitzgerald hosts the most renowned Hollywood parties. The same year, discovering F. Scott's affair with the silent-film actress Lois Moran, Zelda stuffs all her own clothes into the bathtub and sets them afire.

1933 CE: For Pablo Picasso, art augments nature and the artist is a second creator, one unbounded by any law. His paintings are his legacy, his progeny, his immortality. God, he says, is just another artist. And also, 'Everything is a miracle. It's a miracle we don't melt in the bath.'

1984 CE: When his fishing trawler sinks, Guðlaugur Friðþórsson swims six hours in the North Atlantic off the coast of the Westman Islands. Two fellow fishermen die of hypothermia, but 'the miracle man' somehow survives the cold and the Kraken by talking to *múkki*, seabirds, and unknowingly relying on his seal-like fat, found later to be three times thicker than usual for humans. Finally navigating the cliffs and crawling up onto an ancient lava field, Friðþórsson walks barefoot over two kilometres of terrain. His soles turn to ribbons that unravel across pumice humps of molten rock. He finds a bathtub meant to trough sheep and punches a hole through its ice, finally plunging his face in the fresh water to drink.

1999 CE: In a British Columbia time-share, Diana Yano drowns her five-year-old daughter and her three-year-old son to heaven.

2000 CE: *Pity the bathtub its forced embrace of the human form.*

2002 CE: An eccentric en route to his own wedding travels over one thousand kilometres from Odessa to Kyiv in a motorized bathtub. In the vicinity of Uman, he is trapped for two hours on the roadside, swarmed by a storm of stag beetles.

2003 CE: In his documentary *My Architect*, Nathaniel Kahn explores the secret life of his father, world-renowned architect Louis Kahn, who maintained three different families with three different women. Nath, revealing the truth of his paternity for the first time, lays bare his father's social delinquency, but also honours the artist and visionary. In one section, viewers navigate footage of the Trenton Bath House in New Jersey, a pivotal design Kahn credits as a turning point in his career – 'from this came a generative force which is recognizable in every building I've designed since.' Nath pairs the Bath House with an archival audio track of his father:

A work of art is not a living thing that walks or runs, but the making of a life. That which gives you a reaction. To some it is the wonder of man's fingers. To some it is the wonder of the mind. To some it is the wonder of technique. And to some, how real it is. To some, how transcendent it is. Like the Fifth Symphony, it presents itself with a feeling – that you know it, if you've heard it once. And you look for it. Though you know it, you must hear it again. Though you know it, you must see it again. Truly a work of art is one that tells us Nature cannot make what Man can make.

2007 CE: Tatsuya Ichihashi rips out the bathroom fixtures in his Tokyo sky-rise flat. After beating Lindsay Ann Hawker to death with an amputated faucet, he buries her in a bathtub of sand on his balcony. Weeks later police find her, right fingertips exposed, pinned by weather to the rim.

2011 CE: Two road workers recline in a makeshift hot tub atop a fire fuelled with ruins from the drowned city of Fukushima.

2014 CE: I need to soak. Gathering my spilt hair from the pillow, I rise from the television news, from the *navalia proelia* on our sheets. Grief isn't an epoch; it's a milieu. In the tub, Mom's waiting, water slipping through the noose at its bottom. Tuberous teats in the faucet's bulb. One damp hand fixed to the hot faucet; fingernails chewn, skin leavened at the quick. It's not quick; the earth turns round on its spit.

3300 CE: The untethered husks of our bathyspheres tub to shore and spa like meteors on a lush rub of beach. Fomenting sleep escapes from the slack jaws of their hatches ajar. No one to breathe; no one to breathe against. My nude feet match the pitching heave of sand, pass the batches of dismembered claws piled like garbage. I only meant to shush you for a node, a nodule in time. Our water births and our burials at sea come to this. *Take my mother, throw her in the ocean. Who should love me, O, like the ocean?* I douche in tsunami; I'm radiant. It's the end of man and I can do whatever I want.

EVIL BRECKEN

Is what you reckon.
Upper lip, brindled. Pubes, lichen.
Brackish armpits; thigh-thickened

chicken. A wank on the way
to other women. Box on a stick;
wake of peckers. Stupid

with bravado yet brutally
forsaken by self. I rut
in her blood past the bracelets.

Fused sex to sex, pixel to pixel,
we sit together, shit together,
brandish our teats

like handkerchiefs, *oink oink*,
muddle in the bristly
bacon of us: wrecking-

ball vulva, this bathetic smile.
These brambly old hands.
Our sandpaper masturbation.

Booze keeps the wounds
clean and the brain
meaner. Brecken,

you're named after a dog.
Brecken, you cuckold
my time. Brecken, whose cock's

in our esophagus?
It sickens me
to take her in the mirror.

That's wrong – I'm not *taking* her.
She's choked me out. Bracken
to my lesser fern.

Or I'm the leather chew
she's breaking in.
Her nightly grinding

buckles the crackling
cheeks, pouches the jowls,
leaves black pudding

beneath the eyes.
Would you liken her
to her daddy? Something

a little manly? Or to the sag
of grandma's hip-sac reflection?
How I'm aching to dissect

the feckless veil of her –
shave her face off
my face, bride

to my suicide.
But I'm too bloody
vain to maim what's visible

above the neckline
and I can't be alone.
Goddammit, don't go.

Don't tell me my self-pity
is a bummer. Don't
leave. Don't say I'm both

the obstacle and the goal.
I'm my own heckler.
Brecken is what?

Freckled? Mulled wine?
Bluff? Slope rise,
hillside, dip, declivity,

depravity? To break?
To shake a feeling?
Mottled, hot, hoochy,

declining. How do you know
what's to your liking?
If you, unsuspecting,

met yourself, would you
recognize your Jekyll's hidden
side? Share a glass?

Dish on childhood neglect?
Finish each other's pretences?
Hook up? Break up?

Bridle the fucker's brio?
Hack through varicose veins
that blacken the calf,

breaching cellulite? No –
I won't *pull myself together.*
I'm my own distraction.

There's a widening gulf
between each brazen
erection of I–I–I,

a whole brood of knockoffs
infecting me. These phantom
pregnancies I'm expecting.

Uterus, barbed. Tubes, *unheimlich.*
Pickled genes; paretic pelvis. *Brr,*
I need protecting ...

Hush, my Brecken, lie down with me.
Lover, lecher, what beckons – your bestie,
penetrant, bloodline, heaven.

I forget the word to make a broom a broom once more.
> – Goethe

Between 1995 and 2013, my mom kept dying and dying and dying. It seemed she'd never finish.

▸▸

Sweep her up, this scarecrow, skirt on a stick. Hydra. Chop her in two, in four, in forty thousand, and her pieces won't lie down. Won't die die.

▸▸

The timeline is recursive. She was only forty when her symptoms first presented and she was treated for menopause, depression, bipolar disorder and, finally, twelve years after we stopped recognizing her personality, and beyond the point when she could understand the diagnosis, we found she had a rare brain condition and that it was deadening.

That Christmas my dad, brother and I spent our holiday in the psychiatric ward. Mom still smoked back then, and we would accompany her onto the six-by-six outdoor patio, an inescapable concrete pad enclosed with a chain-link ceiling. It was –30° C and we huddled out there in the darkness. Were we still a family of four?

Mom would stand in her pyjamas and green, knee-length insulated coat, puffing without remembering how to inhale. Hair forcibly washed, stringy, scraggly, broomstraw. Face: wet-bread white. Disconnected from language, from subjectivity, she still ached for home. She forgot her name, forgot her pronoun: adopted the neuter 'it.'

▶▶

It asks my brother over and over to break it out:

'Take it. Take it to where you have your life.'

▶▶

Before the disease rendered it completely dumb, it was abusive. Exiling me from home, it forbade me from visiting and told me repeatedly that it hated me. It chased my dad with a knife and would sometimes turn on the car in the garage – make him watch while it knelt at the tailpipe, purposely sucking in exhaust.

▶▶

Here's not so much an assortment of ghosts as one ghost in many iterations. You need forty sets of eyes to see her.

In her coffin, a girl. In her coffin, a crone. In her coffin, a new purple dress and a white scarf. In her coffin, stillness, halted weather. A nest of silkworm chewings. In her coffin, claws. In her coffin, I said claws.

▶▶

After his mother's funeral, Roland Barthes began a mourning diary, scraps of thought collected on loose Post-it-sized squares, intending to turn them into a book. He was hit by a laundry van and succumbed to chest injuries before he could refine the manuscript, but the jot notes have been published. His initial entry reads:

> *First wedding night.*
> *But first mourning night?*

I've always intended to write a response to Barthes's *Mourning Diary*, but I'm stuck on the first page. *First* must contain a beginning, but this year my mother died for the forty-thousandth time and I married for the second. I learn, it seems, through repetition: marriage, mourning.

Having never married, Barthes speaks of weddings in the abstract. His mother was the intimate woman in his life and he categorizes the end of their relationship – her death – as an inversion of sexual union. I understand this conflation of the maternal with the erotic: my mother's madness has occupied a space in my self-hatred next to a chain of failed love affairs. I often thought of our estrangement as a breakup.

In English, we have only one word for *love*. Likewise, synonyms for *loss* fall away. I've inherited my mother's decayed vocabulary.

▸▸

I tried lying in bed for a year. I tried cutting myself open.
I tried swimming during riptide in the Bay of Fundy. I
tried a man who threw rocks at me. I tried poverty.

Mother, I wish we were dead together.

Take me. Take me to where you have your death.

►►

I love my husband. We made a suicide pact: no suicide.

►►

When his mother dies, Barthes begins to mourn. Her
passing represents both the commencement and the con-
summation of his grief. Stretching back almost twenty
years, there's no inaugural evening for my grieving. No
christening for the loss of her.

What time was she travelling through those last, mute years?

►►

The sludge smudging the rug black.
The mollusc's grunge her bare feet trudged.
The trail dug between where she drugged
herself and where she slept.

►►

I don't want prettified versions of dementia. The vomitous
stench of permanent hospitalization, the distorted facial
features caused by brain decay, the zombification, the shit
smeared on the walls – I can't match these with trite movie
versions of losing a forgetful, radiant loved one. Gena
Rowlands all silver in a wheelchair.

By the time Mom died, her limbs were willow-thin, skewed unnaturally under blankets. Guppy lips, amoeba face and the violations of vibrating seizure. The mind within her mind, a small doll in the corner of a dark room.

▸▸

I thought I had reconciled my anger. But her cremated remains – the ceramic, tear-shaped urn – stirred up a lake effect of emotions. *Snow pilots blinded by ash.*

We cannot say: *Now, for the first time, her life is over. Now, this first night, we will begin to mourn.*

I married my second husband six months after the death of my forty-thousandth mother. There is no first.

▸▸

There's no crime in this kind of death. It's genes or a fatal confluence of timelines; it's just unlucky. But Joan Didion expresses the guilt that seems always to accompany loss:

> *If the dead were truly to come back, what would they come back knowing? Could we face them? We who allowed them to die? The clear light of day tells me that I did not allow John to die, that I did not have that power, but do I believe that? Does he?*

I haven't kept up with current theories about time, but I don't give a fuck if time is sinuous, simultaneous, infinite. I know only one way forward.

▸▸

She's dead. I confess. Her abuse was the cruellest thing I've endured. Losing her, particularly an imagined *healthy* version of her, the most devastating. She hated me. I confess. She loved me. I'm criminal for defiling her name.

This poem isn't making me feel better. It's no time travel.

►►

Mother, I'm the witch you raised, raising myself up without you.

I tried to tidy you up, but I'll never be done. The forty thousand brooms have overrun.

I forget the word to make Sandy a monster no more.

►►

One night she asks my dad, 'Why don't you have a nick-name for me?'

'Is there something you'd particularly like?'

'I want to be called Magic.'

EPILOGUE

FALLOWTIMES. A grave
math: water running with no
one to take a bath.

NOTES AND ACKNOWLEDGEMENTS

Earlier versions of these poems appeared in the chapbooks *Strung* (JackPine Press, 2005) and *The Art of Plumbing* (above/ground press, 2013); in the broadside *Husha* (above/ground press, 2013); as well as in *Riddle Fence, EVENT, Grain, CV2, Ottawater, The Fiddlehead, PRISM,* The Dusie Blog: Tuesday Poem and the anthology *The Hoodoo You Do So Well.* Many thanks to the editors, and special gratitude to rob mclennan for tremendous support right when I needed it.

This book would not have been possible without generous financial assistance from the Canada Council for the Arts and the Saskatchewan Arts Board.

Thank you to Susan Holbrook for invaluable editorial guidance and to Alana Wilcox, Leigh Nash, Evan Munday, Heidi Waechtler and everyone at Coach House – it's been a dream to live in your house.

The support of friends and family has been a lifeline, evidenced by the fact that many of these poems took shape on the 'house-sitting circuit.' My love to Janie and John Dodds; Brenda Hoffman and Kim Ward; Joan and Joe O'Shea; Courtney Ward and Bill Bobey; Sarah Neville; Susan Sproull and Kim Hancock; Krista and Logan Hancock; Diane and Doug Markle; Lee and Frank Chapelle; and Cindy and Jeff Steeves.

I am indebted to Tyler Brett and Kerri Reid for residencies at the Bruno Arts Bank. I'm also grateful for residencies at the Banff Centre for the Arts and Sage Hill, and to my mentors over the many years it took to get here: John Livingstone Clark, Tim Lilburn, Ross Leckie, Gerry Shikatani, Barry Dempster, Elizabeth Philips, Don McKay and Anne Simpson. The spirit of your guidance is in this book.

►►

Alone at night, / I Sandy the bed paraphrases the refrain of Anne Sexton's 'The Ballad of the Lonely Masturbator.'

Pity the Bathtub Its Forced Embrace of the Human Form is the title of Matthea Harvey's first collection of poems.

Take my mother, throw her in the ocean ... is a mishearing of a line from a song by The Organ.

In at least two places, I stole from Virginia Woolf.

Plumbing and bathing websites across the Googleverse lent text to and influenced the language in 'Notes to Historia Thermæ' and 'The Art of Plumbing.'

►►

'Winter, Frontal Lobe,' is for Dad. Thank you for repeatedly freeing me from under ice.

'Mom's Sisters' Daughters' is for Auntie Brenda and Courtney – the mother and sister in my life.

'The Near Site' is for Jeramy Dodds, tricorne-hat-sporting hunter of the centaur. Thank you dearly for your endless support of my work and your tireless readings of draft after draft.

'Notes to Historia Thermæ,' particularly the Devil's Bathtub, is for Sarah Neville, my eyes and ears on the ground.

'The Art of Plumbing' is for Pascale McCullough Manning and Stewart Cole. For over ten years now, we've been spanning time together – sharing meals, walks, sadnesses, joy. You have inspired me toward better writing and thinking. Stewart, I felt these poems could enter the world only after I'd talked them over and over with you.

'Her Quiet Not Quite Not Her' is for Adrienne Gruber, who always knew it belonged.

'Lag' is for Logan Hancock, my companion in losing and gaining time.

Andrew Markle, you generous, funny, brilliant, adventurous miracle – you're here, in every word.

Mom, we all miss you.

BRECKEN HANCOCK'S poetry, essays, interviews and reviews have appeared in *Riddle Fence, EVENT, CV2, Grain, The Fiddlehead* and *Studies in Canadian Literature*. She is Reviews Editor for *Arc* and Interviews Editor for Canadian Women in the Literary Arts. She lives in Ottawa, Ontario.

Typeset in Aragon and Aragon Sans, from Canada Type.

Printed at the old Coach House on bpNichol Lane in Toronto, Ontario, on Zephyr Antique Laid paper, which was manufactured, acid-free, in Saint-Jérôme, Quebec, from second-growth forests. This book was printed with vegetable-based ink on a 1965 Heidelberg KORD offset litho press. Its pages were folded on a Baumfolder, gathered by hand, bound on a Sulby Auto-Minabinda and trimmed on a Polar single-knife cutter.

Edited by Susan Holbrook
Cover image by Eric White, *The One* (oil on canvas), 2004
Designed by Evan Munday
Author photograph by Andrew Markle

Coach House Books
80 bpNichol Lane
Toronto ON M5S 3J4
Canada

416 979 2217
800 367 6360

mail@chbooks.com
www.chbooks.com